ENLIGHTENED ENTREPRENEURS

ENLIGHTENED ENTREPRENEURS

How to Make an Income Through Impact and Create a Life of Purpose

COREY GLADWELL

Peach Elephant Press

First Printing, 2016

ISBN 978-0-473-36677-3

Peach Elephant Publishing
NonFictionBook.co

CONTENTS

Acknowledgments

This book is dedicated to the millions of souls that have a message to share, that have a heart for helping others – that want real change in the world they live in.

To my family for their love and support –my mother, Cathy, for always believing in me even when I didn't believe in myself and showing me what it takes to be good in the world.

To my father, Steve, for keeping me grounded and focused on just taking the next step.

To my sister, Candice, for the inspiration she has given me and for being my guardian all the years we grew up together.

To my best friend, Amber, for giving me the love I never knew I needed and supporting me through it all.

To my best friend, Spencer, for his encouragement and ability to deepen our shared consciousness together.

To all my friends for their loyalty through the good and the bad.

To all my mentors that have led the way before me and who have been the stepping stone for me to share my message.

And finally to the person right now reading this book.
Don't ever give up, share from your heart. The world
needs to hear your voice!

As Gandhi said – your life is your message.

Introduction

"The purpose of life is the expansion of happiness." - Maharishi Mahesh Yogi

CRUMPLED, TORN DOWN, and destroyed overnight. I had lost everything. I was jobless, carless, penniless, and nearly homeless. Why was I lying here feeling like shit?

They say your early twenties are supposed to be the best years of your life. It is widely accepted that you take risks and are bold in this time of your life, because you have little commitments.

I did everything I was meant to do, took risks, started companies, and made 'the money'.

I had built up my empire from scratch: my nightclub, my restaurant, and my vodka brand. It was all something I used to think was a total success.

Yet here I was – a shell of the man I knew I could be, hollow and exhausted. There was nothing left in my life that seemed to matter anymore. Like a rubber band stretched too thin, I was dangerously close to snapping and breaking beyond any chance of restoration.

The chains had fallen off. I lost any drive that I may have once had. Material wealth was all that existed in my life and when that was not enough, I had nothing.

How did I let this happen? Why was my world disintegrating around me?

Holey socks stolen from neighbors' clotheslines and hand-me-down shirts from Red Cross clothing bins gave me every inspiration I needed to start my businesses and make money in the beginning.

From a destitute, public-benefit-dependent family, I quickly learnt that owning my own business was a way out of the poor lifestyle I was raised in.

This kid-from-welfare mindset early infused in me, the tendency to be solely hyper-focused on money as the only means to success.

And I did it. I made it out of poverty – and much more. I learnt many valuable lessons along the way. A major piece of wisdom I picked up was that the more you know, the more you can make. Knowledge is power. If you know how to run and operate a business, then you can be in charge of the business instead of it being in charge of you. If you know information, then you can sell information. If you know how to create a product, you can sell that product.

I spent a lot of time learning everything I could about business, life, anything I could get my hands on. I read book after book. I absorbed as much knowledge and information as I could, and then I implemented everything I learnt. I was in a position of power and eventually, I was able to share that knowledge with others.

I grew an empire; and then abruptly, I watched it fall. For a time, the businesses seemed to be going great. I was seeing the right metrics and hitting all my targets. Yet, instead of feeling joy and excitement in all these wins, my energy was constantly depleted. The desire to continue the daily grind and implement all the necessary systems to make sure my businesses were running smoothly faded away; no matter how hard I tried, my motivation was gone and the void in my soul could not be filled.

I had learnt so much, but there I was, January 2012, lying in my bed, sadly reflecting. I had everything – more cars, girls, money, friendships, and material success than I thought anyone could ever want; yet I was utterly lost and unsatisfied. At this point, I had given up, sold, or lost everything I had. I was barely more than homeless.

I had been in this state of despair and desolation for months before I started to realize that it was in fact my own set of beliefs and attitude towards making money to blame. The fact that I thought nothing else mattered, as well as my own experience of not feeling fulfilled internally, was the root of my empire's demise.

Then, I asked myself a question that changed it all. It was this:

"Am I the only one in the world, the only one in the universe?"

It was in that moment my mind snapped. There was a lesson I had not yet learnt. I realized it was just me, but not 'Corey Gladwell' me. Me as in this one being – the universe, experiencing itself as itself. I was the universe's eyes to see, its ears to hear, and I was here to fulfil its own desire.

All at once, my heart cracked open, allowing me to feel this unconditional love for everything and everyone on this planet. I was one with the bed, one with the walls, one with every person I met. I spent three weeks in this state of unconditional love, this total bliss and oneness with everything.

From emptiness, isolation, and total depression to this surreal bliss, I finally saw that there was no such thing as separation. There was no such thing as duality, and in reality, all was one. That was what really changed my life trajectory. I stopped concentrating on that one golden prize: money. Instead, I wanted to give back to the world because I knew the world was myself.

When I realized that the world is truly a reflection of me, and that everything is me, I changed my focus of business, and how I was going to live my life. Business would now not be separate from spirituality; as my life would not be separate from my work. If I were ever going to get into business again, it would be to add value to other people's lives. I would come from a place of meaning and purpose. I would give people a transformation and fulfil them, because to fulfil them would be to fulfil myself.

This realization set me on a path. I now deeply understood that the longer you do not live out what you are truly here in this world to do, the more unsatisfied, empty and less fulfilled you become. This is important to comprehend. Not only can this damage your mental and emotional wellbeing but your physical health too. Your body will give you signs. It will get sick. It will develop problems. Not living true to yourself destroys your life and fills it with catastrophes. This is the universe's way of nudging you in the right direction, telling you to wake up and follow your true calling.

If you wake up every morning dreading going to a job you hate - one that you do just to pay the bills - your life will be unfulfilling and unsatisfying. There will always be a hint of emptiness in the back of your mind, knowing there is something else you are supposed to be doing.

That's the very least. It can easily - and often does - go as far as sickness or divorce, or waking up at the age of 65 with a deep regret. I feel lucky that I was able to hit that moment of regret at 25 because I realized that the financial security, or the safety of working for someone else, was not quite enough.

You can see what is emerging in place of the more traditional view of 'get a job, have security, get a pay check' with this next generation. You can see the dissatisfaction with the older generations. You see the itch with younger generations; people want real life changing results. People want real experiences.

The old way of entrepreneurship was to 'create a product and sell it'. Now, many people are in a search for meaning. Not just entrepreneurs, but the customers themselves. Customers want to know why you're doing what you are doing and what your motive is. Entrepreneurs want purpose in their mission, adding meaning to their service or product and how they serve their customers. You want fulfilment. Even if you make money, you make a product, or you have job, you still want meaning in your life.

That search for meaning is everywhere, and it causes a deep dissatisfaction, because where you are is not where you want to be. There is an everlasting sense of following your passion and your purpose, and bringing it into business. You want to be able to take risks and really get a reward out of it.

However, if you are one of those people who follow their passion and purpose, and bring it into business, the rewards are endless. True fulfilment. Real joy. You will wake up extra early – two hours before you have to – and you will be excited to start what you used to call work; but now it no longer feels like work. You feel like your life is harmonious. You do not feel a separation between what you are supposed to do and what you want to do.

Those things all merge: your work, your family, your business. Everything becomes one thing, and you can truly have that complete wholeness that we all long for.

In the course of this book, I will insert summaries and action steps at the end of each chapter for you to take the knowledge you are gaining and make it a reality. I will make reference to important exercises in the bonus chapter at the end of this book. Information without action is meaningless. Hence, what I truly want for each individual I connect with is for him or her to change, to grow, to evolve, and to enlighten themselves.

My mission in life is to leave every person I meet – whether personally or through my work – better off than when I found them. That is my goal with this book. That is my goal with everything I do. My wish is for you to find your purpose, find your mission, carry a message, and deliver a transformation to those you meet. In life and in business, I imagine a world full of enlightened entrepreneurs living with purpose. A world full of people spreading a message of love and peace, producing transformations in their clients and friends, and living in enlightenment in action.

PART I

Introspection

in·tro·spec·tion

/ˌintrəˈspekSH(ə)n/

noun

The examination or observation of one's own mental and emotional processes.

CHAPTER I

Discover Enlightenment

"Life supports that which supports life."
– Tony Robbins

S IMPLY PUT, THE AWAKENING I went through and that I want to share with you is about becoming enlightened. Enlightenment means to know the world is simply a reflection of you. It is you. From every person that you encounter, everything you see on TV or the Internet or your day-to-day life – everything in this world is you. Money, success, fame, fortune, health, happiness, all the positive, all the negative, is simply a reflection of your state of being.

Enlightenment is being at one. Duality is the world of separation. Duality is the cause of all the suffering in the world and in your world. When I speak of duality, I mean the idea that there is a separate self – the idea that anything at all is separate.

Before we continue, it is important to note that words themselves can be misleading. Different words are supercharged with various meanings; they come with baggage and associations which are different for different people. I encourage you to let go and be open-minded with the words used here. What is more important is understanding the concepts and the principles being discussed. There's no need to get hung up on terms or the words themselves. You can call it what you want. I will continue to refer to this concept of oneness as 'enlightenment'.

Enlightenment would be to accept that each of us are part of a collective; we are one. If this can be accepted, then we would end our suffering; because to kill our planet, suppress women or minorities, decide not to feed the hungry or shelter the homeless, is all truly only injuring ourselves.

There is no real person as a separate self. The idea that Corey Gladwell exists is an illusion I have created to continue feeding my own ego.

Once you understand that the separate self is simply an illusion, and that the true self is all 7.4 billion of us experiencing simultaneously, then you will no longer feel the need for greed. You will no longer support the infliction of suffering on others because that would mean you are causing yourself suffering.

Killing the planet is killing yourself. You would always want to help others live full, healthy, happy lives. No one would consciously harm him- or herself; kill him- or herself; starve him- or herself; let him- or herself suffer, or be homeless.

That only comes from confusion in the mind. The world is currently confused because it is doing exactly those things to itself.

This is mirrored on a microscopic level; cells believing they are separate turn inwards and start killing the body, causing cancer. The human being has done the same and lost its oneness with the body of the planet. It thinks it is its own separate self.

You may be part of the arm and I may be part of the ear, yet we are one body. Individuality is fine as long as we remember we're part of one body.

In the end, we are the universe experiencing itself as itself. If we remember this, we cease to cause pain to ourselves.

When you wake up to that and believe it as the truth, you will realize that everything you do in this world is simply to help yourself, because you and the world are one. By helping others, you are healing yourself. All is one; and when you can realize this, there is a sense of peace, acceptance, and love that you may never experience without enlightenment.

Attaining Enlightenment

I cannot say exactly how you will, or can, reach your own state of enlightenment. Finding that sense of oneness could happen in a moment, or it could happen over a time. It is a deeply personal journey.

Though I can explain the principles and benefits of enlightenment, it is a realization that you have to come to yourself – and everybody does this in a different way.

However, I can give you the basic premise of where to start. It is an exercise that helped me greatly – a simple habit to form that will get you ever closer to that state. It can be likened to a form of meditation *(If you are new to meditation, please refer to the bonus chapter for an introduction).*

Take something you are extremely grateful for and dive into it. Really deeply explore that gratefulness. Enlightenment in its most basic form is extreme gratitude.

Take that thing you are extremely grateful for – whether it is a person, an experience, a feeling, or some item you have, whatever it is that you are extremely grateful for – and really feel and experience deep gratitude for that person, place, or thing.

When you get into a state of gratitude, extend it to everything that exists; to every person, every place, and every part of the world. Encompassing everything as one thing allows you to realize that all the gratitude that you have is really for everything that exists. It is there that you will find yourself in a state of enlightenment, where you can be grateful for everything as one.

Purpose of Enlightenment

Why, though? Why must you immerse yourself in this gratitude? Why even bother trying to reach enlightenment? Achieving enlightenment is no small effort, so why should you use your energy in this way. It will require dedicated time and effort, but like all great things in life, the outcomes are a thousand fold worth the effort. It is a hugely significant thing to be enlightened, arguably essential, as being in a state of enlightenment means the end of your suffering. It is the end of the illusion of separation and the understanding that helping the world is truly helping yourself. When you come from a place of separation, of duality, you come from a 'me versus them' mentality. You exist in a state of competition, with an apparent need to beat someone at something or to win over something.

An attitude like that, one that predisposes you to be at odds with the world and with yourself, causes conflict within you, because you are never satisfied. You never come from a place of true gratitude. You are always in a position of suffering because you always think it is me versus them. When you come from a place of enlightenment and you work from this place, you realize there is no separation.

You understand that the person you are helping is really yourself, so you want to serve them in the best manner possible. You want to give others a transformation. You want to take them to better places and present them with opportunities to operate at higher levels than they have ever dreamed they could. You desire to give them everything you have because you know that to heal them, to make them whole, is to make yourself whole. There is a sense of unity, a sense of oneness in that. There is no more duality or competition.

Entrepreneurship

Your goal as an entrepreneur is ultimately to give or create solutions for people's problems. A basic textbook definition of an entrepreneur is 'someone who takes on greater risk in hopes of great reward'. That is the foundation: that you need to take on the risk that the normal, corporate job people would not take.

Being an entrepreneur is not just that though. It is a way of life. You are a content creator. You are a maverick in the business world. You are the person that pushes life forward with new ideas, new inventions, and innovations. It is to be in charge of your business and to be in charge of your life.

There are the obvious benefits to entrepreneurship, the ones that mean that you do not have to show up to work the next day because your business is running itself for you. You live in charge of your life and business.

However, even though you do not *have* to go to work, there is not a day where you do not *want* to go to work, because you love your job, the way you earn an income! It is a whole way of life; there is no more separation between what you are doing and your work. Those things become one. The risk and the unknown becomes a part of who you are as a person.

Being an entrepreneur is so special and unique, because you are in control of your own destiny. If you want something in life, you can go out and create it. You can come up with an idea to solve any problem. You can create the income and the lifestyle you want. You have total control over your own destiny; that is why being an entrepreneur, and taking charge of your life, should be encouraged.

Always remember that entrepreneurship has been glamourized. It is not always easy. Talk to any entrepreneur in the trenches and you soon realize it is hard work day in and day out – and it never stops. It is not always this 'travelling laptop office, thirty days until you can retire on passive income' life that everyone seems to portray it as. You are going to have challenges, and you are going to have real hurdles.

You really have to embrace the unknown, more so than any other person or career.

However, just being on the entrepreneurial journey will not do. Even if you are taking all the right steps in your journey to becoming an entrepreneur, but are not following your passion – that is, what you truly care about – you will run into the ground.

Enlightened Entrepreneur

As I have learnt, it is not enough to simply be an entrepreneur. It is not sustainable to be purely money-driven. You will grow weary and tired as I did. This is why you must combine the two. This notion is the foundation of this book's teachings.

When you are an enlightened entrepreneur, everything changes. You know that you are helping yourself. You realize that everything that you are doing for your business is really to solve a problem for yourself. Your clients are actually versions of you.

When you solve a problem for them, when you help them succeed, you are helping yourself succeed.

With that, you have a never-ending passion to serve others and to serve yourself. This is sustainable and life-giving. It is the end of 'work' as we know it. There is no more work because your work becomes your life, and your life becomes your work. These merge into one thing. There is no more compartmentalization in your life. You begin to feel much more alive when you do not separate the activities in your life. It is no longer 'work' and 'leisure', but both simply become your life. The time you are spending is your life, which is why it is really important to be doing something that you love.

Ultimately, each of you must choose whatever path awakens you from the inside out. That is what an enlightened entrepreneur's path is. You do not have to call it that, but everyone should have true freedom to live his or her internal as the external. Whatever you want to call it, whatever name or title you give it, design a lifestyle that awakens you from the inside.

Discover Enlightenment

Meditation:

- What am I truly grateful for?
- Can I encompass all that exists in life as this one thing?
- Can I feel profound gratitude for all that exists?
- Meditate on gratitude, appreciation and love for my work and life.

Action Steps:

- Meditate for 10-20 minutes daily
- Write out your life as an enlightened entrepreneur.
- How would you think, feel, and act as an enlightened entrepreneur?

CHAPTER 2

Limiting Beliefs

"The only thing standing between you and your goal is the bullshit story you keep telling yourself as to why you can't achieve it."
— Jordan Belfort

WHEN I WAS BUILDING MY BUSINESSES, I continuously held myself back from making a certain amount of money. In my mind, I thought that the more money I wanted to make, the more time I would have to spend making it. I kept myself at a ceiling of success and financial independence because I believed it would require more time. And that just wasn't true. When I broke that particular limiting belief, I was able to progress past those financial limits and have more free time while making more money.

What Is A Limiting Belief?

Any idea or belief system ingrained in your mind that holds you back from living fully is a limiting belief. Because like Henry Ford said,

"Whether you think you can, or you think you can't – you're right".

We set our own 'having' level – what we believe is possible to achieve. What we have to do is change that belief in order to have more.

Think of it like a thermostat. If you set the air conditioning in a house to 67 degrees, your air con will spend all its time working hard to bring the house temperature up to 67 degrees. Once it accomplishes this, it will stop. More so, if the temperature in the house rises above 67 degrees, it will quickly do all it can to keep it at 67 degrees.

Most people's internal thermostats are set to 'have enough money to buy food, cover rent, a decent car and drinks on the weekends'. Unfortunately, this is a low setting; there is so much more to be had. What is worse is that if they do achieve more than this, they will often unknowingly self-sabotage to bring themselves back down to their comfortable set 'temperature' – because that is where they have set their thermostat. This is our 'having level'.

Major Limiting Beliefs

A common example of a major limiting belief that many people in our society today have, is around success. Many people think that they are scared to fail, when really they are scared to succeed.

When you are successful, you must take on full responsibility for your life and for those that you serve. That responsibility on-boarding process is intimidating and scares many people off because it means you are the architect of your whole life. You are to be held 100% accountable for everything in your life. There is a huge fear of accountability that limits people from truly having success in their life.

I had a limiting belief that I had to achieve a certain status and level of success in life in order to feel free from pressure. Once I accepted the fact that success was who I was - not a certain job, a level of achievement or an amount of money - that was when I truly became successful. It was the end of seeking approval for me.

Examine why you are not where you want to be. What would you have to believe is possible to achieve the life that you want? When you think of having the life that you want, what are the fears that creep up? Usually, there is some kind of fear and we jump to conclusions like:

"Oh well, if I build a business that provides the income I want, then I will have to give up all my family time."

These fears are all make-believe. They are all belief systems that do not serve you – and they are not true. You have never experienced that life, so what are these fears based on. The first step to overcoming your limiting beliefs is examining the fears that you have about your ideal life.

If you think that because you attained a certain house, car, job, business, or amount of income, you will have fulfilment and feel successful, then you need to let go. When you let go of the idea that you need to own this or achieve that, then you can have true fulfilment.

You are free right now in this moment. You have all the success you will ever want right now. When you realize that life is you, that you are life, and that everything you want to achieve is already within you, then there is no separation between you and success.

Vulnerability & Identity

As entrepreneurs, we inherently open ourselves up to a lot of risk. Our wellbeing, that is, putting food on the table, depends upon the project we are working on and its success. There is a possibility our project may fail, and so we leave ourselves open and rather vulnerable.

Vulnerability is important as entrepreneurs and it is an integral part of everyday life for us. We risk our ideas, our vision, and constantly run the risk of being utterly wrong. Our vulnerability and the risks we take are constantly in a dance together, carefully balancing each other. To be vulnerable means to be open, such that anyone can see who you truly are. You are open about what you truly want.

It is also essential to realize that you are not defined by the success or outcomes of putting your ideas into practice, or the things that you create and put out in the world. If your product, service, or idea fails, you do not need to take on that failure as a persona, or even feel like a failure yourself. Remember, there is always a trial and error process; your products or services will not be 100% perfect from the get-go.

People tie too much of what they are creating to who they are as a person. They think that if it fails, therefore, they fail. You must let go of failure as your identity by allowing vulnerability into your life and realizing you will have tons of failure before you have success. You are not that failure; your idea was just not something that was ready to succeed. Your idea may come back later, it may succeed at a different time, but it was not ready yet.

To be vulnerable, you have to be open to people's criticism and judgment. When you pull back the curtain and examine what is really going on, you will discover that it is actually just you judging yourself. You are holding yourself back because you are afraid of your own self-judgement.

Nothing anyone can say to you can ever really affect you unless you already believe it about yourself. When something offends you, it is because some part of you believes it to be true already. Something within you agrees with the comment the person is making. When you let go of self-judgement, of taking things personally, of believing that you are your ideas, then you are free to create without limits. Nothing anyone can say can negatively affect you when you reach this place. Their own self-limiting beliefs of what is possible is responsible for their judgement of you.

When I started my first Facebook fan page, I grew it to 10,000 people within 4 months – and you have to know that when you get to that many people, there will be negativity.

Most of the comments were positive, but as the page grew, there was obviously more opportunity for negative comments to surface. People would say hurtful things or argue trivially and without consideration of anyone else's viewpoint, but I knew everything they said was only really a reflection of themselves. It was because of something inside themselves, an issue they had not accepted, or a problem they had not been able to deal with appropriately, which they then mirrored onto me.

When you can access your vulnerability, you will learn that nothing can really hurt you unless you let it, and so you can prevent yourself from feeling as if you are failing. You must acknowledge that you are on a journey to success; you are continuously trying and erring to improve your idea, service, or product.

The goal is not to prove anything to anyone. Adopt this attitude and you will find that no one can really harm or damage who you are. You cannot fail unless you believe you are failing. Being vulnerable -

allowing yourself to try, and potentially fail, in order to succeed - frees you up to be able to do, create and have anything you want in life.

Encouraging this vulnerability stops you from thinking you have to be perfect, and in turn, you will not die from perfectionism. Many of us struggle with the eternal pursuit of perfection, of needing things to be exactly a certain way before we ever try. By doing that, we waste so much time and so many valuable lessons because we never go out and implement.

Taking action is the one thing that will lead you to any kind of success, and fear of taking action is what will ultimately hold you back. Actually doing and going through the process of failure is the only step you need to take to really unveil where your true successes lie.

Playing Small

You will always end up playing small if you don't embrace vulnerability. You will never want to others to see the real you. You might join a group online, buy a course, or read a book, but you will never take action. You will avoid stepping out into the limelight because you will always be afraid of failing. You will be afraid of others seeing you for who you truly are. You immerse yourself in learning more and more in order to feel better about hiding. Your fear of being vulnerable, of everyone else seeing you for who you truly are and what you want will direct you to a life where you hide your true potential.

When you let go of the fear of being seen by others, the fear of being wrong and the fear of failing, you will acquire more opportunities to play big. Only when you play big are you ever truly able to succeed in life.

Playing small - not allowing yourself to access your vulnerability - will keep you stuck where you are for an indeterminate amount of time. You will never launch, never go for your dreams, and never try. Alternatively, if you do try, you will only try enough to reach a point where others cannot fully perceive you. You stay in your comfort zone, stuck behind the curtain so no one can ever see you and criticize you. That way, you will always have an excuse:

"Oh well, I wasn't really trying to succeed; I didn't really want to become that successful. I only wanted to make $50,000."

Now, there's nothing wrong with making $50,000; however, you do need to examine why your goal is $50,000 or whatever amount you have set it. If you are only staying at a certain level because you are afraid of jumping, of becoming bigger and grander than you are right now, you need to reassess.

On the flip side, playing big gives you access to all the unlimited possibilities life has to offer. There is an abundance of business contacts, ways to launch, ways to diversify and to grow your business that you can have access to if you open your mind to being visible, to stepping into the unknown and being unafraid to fail. Playing big will allow you to be aware of these opportunities. They were always there right in front of you, but you just could not notice them when you were playing small.

When I first got into business, I stayed in learning mode for far too long, always thinking there was just one more thing I had to learn, do or try before I could implement, take action and launch. The notion that there was always just one more thing to know and perfect held me back for months, even years, because I thought there was always something else I didn't know. I finally realized that there will always be things I do not know, but I have to try to implement with what I do know.

Once I finally learnt this and started doing instead of just absorbing more information, I realized that I knew so much more than I thought. Trying, failing, and implementing, are the only ways to fully grasp and understand your life and business' biggest lessons.

Psychology of Success

There is only one way to come close to what you define as success, and that is by actually taking action and doing. Success is the ability to experience what you love. If what you love is your work, then hustling and growing your business is success. If what you love is your family, then spending plenty of quality time with your loved ones is success. If what you love is simply creation, then having the freedom to create more is success. Doing what you love is the ideal of success no matter what form it comes in.

Success does not have to be a million dollars in the bank; it does not have to be an 8-figure business. If that is what you happen to love, then that is what you should do. Success is doing what you love on a more regular basis and not having separation between work and life, or between vacation and your regular life.

"You need to build the life that you do not want to escape from." as Seth Godin said. You can make it so that what you truly love can fill your everyday experiences, which is what you need to live a life that is in alignment with who you truly are.

So, what holds us back from having this success? Our self-inflicted limits to our own success are our internal beliefs. You might think that life needs to show up in a certain way for you to have what you want. Part of the glasses you wear blinds you from seeing all the varied options right in front of you.

You already have everything you need to have success in your life at this moment. There is nothing more you need to add to yourself, nothing more to become to have success. Sure, you can always become more in order to have more success, but right now, in this moment, you can experience success. All you need to do is let go of those limiting beliefs.

At one point in my career, I was stuck at making $30,000 a year, and I would only slowly increase my salary a few dollars at a time. For the longest time I believed that if I wanted a higher income, I would have to work more hours to create that income. I was steadfast in the notion of 'put an hour in, get a fixed dollar amount out'. When my belief about money and success changed, I realized I could have more and work less. I realized that success and money are who I am.

I am all the money in the world. I am all the success in the world. I knew I could have as much money as I wanted and could work whatever number of hours I chose. That whole paradigm in my mind shifted, and suddenly, I went from $30,000 to

$50,000, then to $100,000, and soon to $250,000. My income increased 10 times more than I ever could imagine while working less hours per week. All because my idea of what it took to be successful changed in my mind.

Allowing the money and the time to come into my life was simply a mindset modification I had to make. I had to first accept that the sort of time and money I was dreaming of was possible, before I could fully integrate it into my life.

Tony Robbins's mom wanted him to be a truck driver. She thought it was a safe, secure job. It was twice as much as Tony's dad was capable of making, and she thought that was the perfect dependable, risk-free career path.

It was not until Tony found Jim Rohn that he realized there was so much more out there. He was only then able to accept the amount of success he has now grown into. If you watch the story of Tony's life, you can see jumps of him accepting more success into his life and becoming more successful. The amount of success he was able to accept into his life was the gateway to him actually achieving that level of success.

Success Limits

Breaking your success limit comes back to why being enlightened is important in entrepreneurship. There will be no more separation between you and the life, the time, the money, or the experience you desire, once you fully acknowledge that all that exists is simply you. These things are you and they are yours to have anytime.

When you can combine the world as yourself and be grateful for the whole world as a reflection of yourself, then you can stop feeling as if you must get somewhere or achieve something to have the money or success of your ideal life. You realize it is yours right now – that is the shortcut to getting your dream life right now.

Breaking free from your limiting beliefs requires some internal work. It may not always be easy, but you can always do it. Listed below in the action steps to take is the first thing you must do: write down what you believe. Once you write down everything you believe about life, love, business, success, philosophy and existence, then you should write down the complete opposite of that belief. Allow that opposing belief to be just as true to you. This can be difficult for many people, because like others, we have all become addicted to our beliefs. We are certain that our beliefs are the truth. We believe that it is how the world works and that it is how everyone should believe. To discard this belief is difficult, but on the other side is where freedom exists.

Future Pacing

Another practice I have used that, again, we will review in the summary action steps of this chapter, is future pacing your life. It is a way of breaking free from your current limiting beliefs.

Imagine you are in a year, 5 or 10 from now. Imagine your life worked out exactly how you always wanted it to. Imagine you have created, done, and accomplished all that you ever wanted in life and business. How do you feel? Who have you became? What is your life like now that you have done it all?

Writing out the story of your life as if it has already happened, and then going into a feeling of profound gratitude for it, is the key to pulling you into this future. The future, the past, the present, it is all one moment. You can access it at any time.

Allow yourself to be your future self, with your future life in this current moment. Feel profound gratitude for it as if it has already happened and watch your life change.

Summary 2
Limiting Beliefs

Meditation:

- What do I need to believe in order to allow what I want to be seen as?
- How would my life look if I believe success is who I am?
- What belief about myself or my life is limiting me from my experience?
- Meditate on gratitude for your future life as if it was the past.

Action Steps:

- Spend 10-20 minutes in the above meditation.
- Write down all your beliefs.
- Write down the complete opposite belief to your current beliefs.
- Accept fully that the opposite of what you currently believe is also just as true.
- Write the story of your life in past tense as if your success has already happened.

- How did it feel to experience that success? What changed about you back then to give you that success? How good does it feel to know you already experienced the success you want?

CHAPTER 3

Your Unique Purpose

"He who has a why to live for can bear almost any how."
— Friedrich Nietzsche

"Nothing is more creative... nor destructive... than a
brilliant mind with a purpose."
— Dan Brown

EVERY ONE OF US HAS A MISSION to follow in
life; something that feels bigger than a core
selfish drive, and encompasses an experience that will
truly fulfil you. This mission is your purpose – the
reason you are here on this earth.

If you never find your unique purpose, you will
always experience a feeling of wandering. Many
people get lost eternally wandering through life. We,

as humans, are meaning-making machines, so we try to find purpose in our everyday existence. There is so much purpose in just being alive.

If you do not have a purpose in your business, then the time you spend building it will always feel like work, like a job. You will age more rapidly, wear out faster and get sick more often. You will end up causing more damage to your relationships and finances because you will feel the separation between your work and your life.

When you do not have a business driven by your specific and unique purpose, you can suffer irreparably on every level.

I lost sight of my purpose when running my multi-million-dollar businesses. I felt empty, alone, and like nothing honestly mattered. Every milestone I managed to reach brought me little fulfilment because I did nothing in line with my purpose. It was a meaningless drive just to chase material success.

When purpose does not drive your business, you will not have the passion, the excitement, the energy, and the drive necessary to motivate you day in and day out. You will never be able to get up extra early and easily work for it because your 'work' will not be in alignment with what you truly want. It will absolutely feel like a job.

I had all the money, attention, women, cars and the clothes – yet none of that mattered. None of this material wealth was enough because I was not following something that was truly in my heart.

I escaped the monotony of feeling as if I had to work every day for the rest of my life when I finally did discover what my purpose was and started basing my business around that. I felt motivated to get up extra early and did not feel like there was any separation in my life. Everything became one. I became a constant creator. I was just creating content, giving, and sharing what really helped me. Those that I shared with and taught benefitted immensely and I finally began my passion business.

From then on, when I saw problems in life, I was just able to solve them without having to struggle or ever feel like I was not in control. At last, I felt like my life was my own, and that everything I did had meaning and mattered. My whole life and business was full of my purpose.

The success was not all emotional and mental. The more I followed my purpose and my passion, the more financial returns I gained. I went from being nearly homeless, to finding my purpose and getting ten times the money back.

I grew more loving relationships with all those close to me – my family, friends, and spouse. Opportunities to feature on TV and on podcasts presented themselves, and I became a bestselling author.

These achievements are just the beginning! The compound effect and exponential growth that comes from following your purpose is immeasurable. There is no limit to what could happen once you truly align with your authentic self.

Discover Your Passion

When discovering your own purpose, it is important to make sure the mission is in fact yours, and not an external dogma instilled in you. Another person's purpose for your life is limited and time-bound. It is limited to their vision and their imagination of what they think you are supposed to do. Another person's purpose for your life is time-bound as you will only have a finite amount of motivation to do something for someone else, compared to that which you would do for yourself.

Your own purpose is limitless. It has no expiration date. Your own purpose can evolve and change as you develop and grow. It can become so much more as your imagination expands. Your purpose can advance; you can continually grow with it and into it. Your purpose is self-propelling from the inside out so it will compound on itself and continue to motivate you. Your life's mission will grow and speed up as time goes on, and your motivation and excitement will grow with it.

To discover your own purpose in life, try this simple technique: Take a moment right now to think about the experience you wish to give others. If you could give another person, anyone in the world, a thought, feeling, or an action, what would it be? If you could give them an entire experience, what would that experience be? How would they feel? How would they think? How would they experience life in that moment?

Once you come to a full realization of what it is you would like others to experience above all else, you will see this is what you wish to experience yourself. You will want to give a certain experience to others because you want to experience it yourself. That is your purpose – and by giving it to them, you are living through it yourself.

To give you an example of this, I give others freedom. I give them mental, emotional, and financial freedom. That is what I want others to feel. I want others to feel free in every way. I desire to give them that because that is what I truly want to experience myself. I have always wanted freedom and so I give others freedom.

My sister has always wanted security, so she wants to give other women security. There is an array of examples. My dad always wanted to give people respect because he yearns respect. My best friend, he has always wanted to belong, so he connects others and makes them feel as if they are a part of something bigger.

Linking what you truly want to experience yourself, to what you want to give to others, will cause you to align yourself with a perpetual feeling of being on purpose.

To know for sure what your purpose is, it has to motivate you daily. It has to make you want to get up extra early and work longer hours because you do not feel like you are working at all. You want to share it with everyone. You want to give that experience to every person.

Your purpose is something that you will know is truly aligned with who you are on the inside because it makes you feel whole; it makes you feel complete. Your purpose should make you feel like you could live the rest of your life doing this one thing. If it does not give you that, it is not your purpose. It is not actually what you're meant to do. You will be sure of it when you know that you will do anything to give that to others and to give that to yourself.

SUMMARY 3
Your Unique Purpose

Meditation:

- What do I truly want to experience?
- How would I think, act, feel, do, say and experience?
- What is the experience I want to give to others?
- Is this aligned with my purpose?

Action Steps:

- Meditate on the above for 10-20 minutes
- Write out the experience you want to share with others
- Write out the experience you want to have for yourself

PART 2

Beneficence

Be·ne·fi·cence

/bəˈnefəs(ə)ns/

noun

Action that is done for the benefit of other people; to help prevent or remove harms or to simply improve the situation of others.

CHAPTER 4

Content & Creativity

"I never made one of my discoveries through the process
of rational thinking"
— Albert Einstein

THE FIRST STEP ONCE YOU KNOW what
experience it is that you want share with others,
what your true purpose in life is, is to think about
what transformation it is that you would like to give
your clients. This might stem from what you have
previously identified as a transformation you wanted
to see in yourself, that you might have successfully
accomplished. You can teach the process you
underwent to others!

A transformation is what you should be selling, giving and creating. It should be something that takes your client from point A to point Z. This could be a mental, emotional, financial, or physical revolution.

For example, if I am putting someone through my enlightenedentrepreneursacademy.com course, the person will know, by the end of it, that he or she could do what I have done. This is because I have led them through the transformation that I have already gone through. They can now be a published author, or coach, or create an online course. My clients know that when they complete everything I have set out for them in the course, they could have all of those things listed above, depending on their determination, and how much action they are willing to take. I have promised them a transformation by the end of it, and if I am not delivering that transformation, then obviously, I should not be selling that kind of product or service.

Identifying the transformation you have already been through is vital, because that is what you are able to give your clients.

The Gift of Transformation

Begin by identifying any big problem you have struggled with, that others might have too. Ask yourself these questions:

- What have the hardest times in my life been so far?
- What are the things that other people always say I am good at?
- What did I previously complain about, that I no longer complain about?
- How have others described your changing personality from previous years?

If you were able to find a successful solution that helped you overcome a specific problem, and you think others suffer from this problem too – you have just found the transformation you can give others.

We need to package this transformation in order to deliver it to someone else. There are many ways to package your transformation: online courses, programs, live events, masterminds, or retreats – there are many kinds of delivery systems to choose from.

Content Creation

This brings us to creating content. Essentially, content is the material that you will deliver to your clients – this provides them the transformation you want to give. This is the first step in building the product or service that will fulfil your purpose as an Enlightened Entrepreneur.

As far as the medium, we are aiming for whichever medium the type of people you are serving are most familiar with. Content can be delivered in various ways: text, e-mail, verbally, through a live event or video, or a combination of all those. It could either be recorded or in person.

This content should ideally come from your real life experience. A heart-centered entrepreneur should firmly believe in delivering content that addresses situations that you have actually experienced yourself, or ones that you are very familiar with.

To ensure that your content is original and of the highest quality, what you create should come from the things that have genuinely helped you solve the problem. It could be based on something that you have been taught before or something you are certified in, but you need to be certain that whatever you are presenting will absolutely give the result you are promising. That is how both you and your client reading, watching, or hearing your content will know it is high quality – everything has been tested and confirmed.

What if someone else has done the testing for me? I have seen them achieve great results using the method I want to teach; can't I just go off their results? In short, no. Just because someone else has done it, does not mean you can do it. There is no substitute for experience. Either you prove it yourself, or you take on a beta-tester and have them test-run it as a client. Be certain the client can get the results before you try and sell this transformation.

If you do not have some kind of testing or evidence of your own proven result, then you should not sell or market your product as a 100% guarantee. However, if you have not proven it for yourself, it is still in the testing phase.

The amount of content you must create wholly depends on what you are selling. There are no defined rules - but less is more. It is wise to include the minimum amount of information needed to give your customers their transformation. You do not need to have everything you have ever learnt in there. You only need to present the information that applies to the transformation you want to give. Ultimately, that means no fluff.

It is usually best to think of the content you provide as enough to deliver the transformation that you are promising, but broken down into bite-sized sections.

If you are still curious on length, here are some general guidelines I have seen from the industry:

- If undertaking a live event, then do a two-day or three-day event.
- If an online course, then content is generally broken up into five to eight modules.
- If providing a coaching program, they are usually structured by having weekly phone calls.
- If a group mentorship, these group calls may be bi-weekly.
- Others run a yearly mastermind meetup.

It depends on what kind of transformation you want to give; what it takes and what you are charging. Is it a hundred-dollar course or a ten-thousand-dollar course? If your client is paying ten thousand dollars, they may not be very thrilled if your course is provided through email (not to say that isn't possible!)

Product Pricing

While we are on the topic of how much your course costs, let us address how to decide what it is you should be charging for your offering. This choice is obviously completely yours; your offer could range from $9.95 up to $99,995 or more. The types of results you are offering your client will give you the best indication of the worth of your product or service – and therefore it's price point. Often, you will realize you are selling a high-end product or service, and this means you should charge a premium price.

Do not be afraid of asking what you and your service are worth! If the price you have decided on frightens you, then go back to the action steps and meditations on limiting beliefs and work through them with this limitation in mind. There are thousands of people charging $100,000 or more for their programs, so do not dismiss any number, thinking of it as impossible.

Typically, there are only two frequencies of client payment: charging for your service monthly or a one-off fee. Here are some typical price models:

- Membership Site at $19.95/month
- Online Course at $997-$1997 for a one-time fee
- Coaching Program at $2,500-$25,000 for a one-time fee
- Mastermind at $100,000 for a one-time fee

Make sure you take into consideration how much personal time you will have to invest to give them that result. If it takes more of your personal time, then be sure to add that in. You may offer an information product that you make once; for example, a course on your area of expertise. In this model, you make all the content and upload it onto your chosen platform, and then your clients can go through it at their own time and pace. This means you can set that service up on autopilot, as you do not really have to do much more once you create the course, except market it. If this is the case, you can aim for volume and charge a reduced price.

Most beginner entrepreneurs tend to under-charge, more so than anybody else does. They are inclined to believe that they are not yet worth their actual value. Without the outside world validating them, many entrepreneurs - especially enlightened, heart-centered entrepreneurs - undervalue their products/services.

I personally want the highest results for you, as well as your clients, which is why I suggest starting at a higher price point. When you undervalue your product, you not only sell yourself short, but you sell your clients short too. You will end up giving less value than you would if you had sold your product or service at a higher, more fitting price. Not only that, but a lower price point generally means a worse quality of client.

Enlightened - or heart-centered - Entrepreneurs really want to help people. You genuinely want to be of service, but you do not know what to charge for what you are helping with. You might often be tempted give away so much more value for way lesser money because you do not know how to set up a proper business structure to be paid what you are really worth.

The thing is, you are doing a disservice to your clients when you do not charge higher prices, when you do not ask for what you are actually worth. You are not going to deliver as high a quality value and your clients are not going to be as invested in taking the training, the course, the teaching, or the coaching program as serious.

If they are not invested on a higher level, your clients will not be as motivated to produce their own great results. When your clients pay you what you are actually worth, they will be much more committed financially, emotionally and mentally to taking action and really creating results for themselves. It helps your clients accomplish what you were trying to teach in the first place.

To determine your price, think about what it would cost your client if they did not get your help.

Not only financially, but also emotionally, mentally and physically. What would they lose?

I had to consider this when it came to writing this book and building Enlightened Entrepreneurs Academy. Would my ideal client be depressed if they did not live a purpose-filled life? Would they end up in divorce if they were unhappy with their work life? Would they wake up at 65 with a deep regret about their life and life's work? Would they file bankruptcy because they lost motivation to continue growing their business?

On the flip side of that coin, how might their life change if they do work with you? Could they become the next Tony Robbins? The next Bill Gates?

Lay all this out and you will find you can easily determine the cost of your clients not working with you. This will make it easier for you to understand the value you are delivering and price accordingly.

Tapping Into Creativity

In any aspect of business, creativity is a key element. Creativity is simply: the ability to create. It is a muscle that you exercise when solving problems. Creation can be one of the greatest forms of satisfaction.

When you tap into creativity and get in that place of problem solving and seeking out solutions, you can come up with the best answers to life, for yourself and your client's issues.

What makes you an entrepreneur is the ability to solve a problem other people cannot or have not solved. You can see the solution before anyone else can and bring it to life. You can translate it into a book, course, program, or service that you offer. That is the key to business. Business is about knowing something that someone else does not know and how you can help him or her know or understand it.

The emergence of Airbnb was, originally, due to the founders needing extra money. They knew there was a huge issue in San Francisco where hotels were expensive and low value, but extremely in demand. The founders were creative in finding a solution, not only to their lack of money, but also to the city's lack of affordable accommodation. They blew up an air mattress in their studio apartment and charged someone to stay a few nights in their lounge. It worked well and they realized, "Hey, if we can do this with one person, maybe we can do this with more people."

That was the birth of Airbnb. They came up with an entire billion-dollar business.

Take Uber as another classic example. Just like with any business, if you find a gap or a problem in a market, you can find a solution to it. There was an excess of capacity (vacant cars) and a demand for that capacity (people need to get places). Uber found an opportunity. Not only that, but they noticed the lack of taxicab drivers. There was only a specific amount, and that amount did not suffice the needs of a growing San Francisco. They were able to create a company, based around the everyday citizen becoming their own taxi driver and making extra money on the side. It solved multiple problems. The first being the problem of people not having enough income, and the other problem being people not having options to get them home after a night out drinking or around town to sightsee. It solved two problems and created a billion-dollar business as well.

To tap into your own billion-dollar business creativity, meditation is the key. Quieting the mind. Letting go of the limiting filters that cloud your everyday perception. Allowing space for new ideas to come and flow through you. There is an unlimited resource of content and creativity once we get out of our own way. If you, like so many others, consider yourself as analytical or as having that left-brain type mentality, you can be totally caught up in your own thoughts, perceptions, filters, and beliefs. These things can limit you.

Go to a quiet place and clear your mind; whether you need to journal and pour your thoughts out, or just sit in meditation. You can completely empty your mind and allow free-flowing thoughts or ideas to come to you. I have had entire courses come to me through meditation. I have had entire new books come to me during meditation. The fully-fledged outlines, the structure, everything from start to finish, has come to me during an hour of meditation for multiple projects I have worked on. All because I quietened my mind and allowed it to be free, flow openly and tap into where all creativity comes from.

Content & Creativity

Meditation:

- Spend 10-20 minutes in quiet meditation clearing your mind of trying

- Allow yourself to flow with an empty mind and access whatever thoughts come

Action Steps:

- Do the above meditation.

- After the meditation free-flow, write any and all ideas that come to you.

- Do not judge or criticize or try to figure out how this all will happen. Just let yourself write all that comes to you

- After you've emptied your mind on paper, take a moment to organize your thoughts into content then prepare for the next chapters.

CHAPTER 5

Narrowing Your Niche

"Every man has a specific skill, whether it is discovered
or not, that more readily and naturally comes to him
than it would to another, and his own should be sought
and polished. He excels best in his niche - originality
loses its authenticity in one's efforts to obtain
originality."

— Criss Jami

IN ORDER TO AIM YOUR CREATIVITY at solving
precisely the right problems for the right people,
you need to define your niche. A niche is a sub-
category. A smaller market segment within a larger
market. For example, this book could have been
about entrepreneurs only, but instead there is a shift
in focus to enlightened entrepreneurs, a subcategory

of entrepreneurs. You combine these two categories into a smaller sub-category, a smaller segment of a larger whole market. You need to niche down and target a specific target audience.

Narrow Your Niche

The more you niche down, and the smaller the group you find, the easier it is to solve an immediate problem with your solution. You can always extend that and include more people. The more you narrow down, the more defined your audience is, which will make it easier to help solve your audience's specific problem. It also makes it a lot easier to market to them directly.

A great example of narrowing down to a specific niche is Nerd Fitness. They took two categories and combined them into one clear-cut niche. They took people that felt like they were nerds, like they did not really fit in at a gym, and specifically tailored their content and solution to integrate these people into the fitness industry. Nerd Fitness combined the two separate markets, created a specific niche market which they took over, and exploded because of it.

They understood a problem that was in the market, and because they saw that gap, they were able to find a solution to it by combining two different categories into a sub-category. Now they know how to solve their specific audience's pain points a lot better than they could if they were trying to go after only the fitness industry or trying to go after nerds for something completely different.

However, it is possible to niche so far down and target a group that is too small. The more you niche down, the harder it is to find those exact type of people or group. The other thing that is important to remember is that you identify with this group. It is easy to accidentally stop being authentic. Being an Enlightened Entrepreneur is all about being authentic to who you are and what you want to provide to the world.

So, you should niche down just enough to target a specific pinpoint and solve a specific problem, but not so far as to eliminate yourself from including anybody. It is important to start small and then work your way up to more broad examples. You start with a specific niche (group of people) and then you can widen, becoming broader and including more people or groups as time goes on.

This is exactly what Jeff Bezos of Amazon.com did. Though they are well-known as the "Everything Store" now, they weren't always. Their first niche (or specific market/group of people) was books. They wanted to revolutionize how books were bought and first made the ultimate online bookstore. Only after that was a success did they expand who they were serving and open up additional avenues, broadening their niche.

The issue is you cannot sell to everyone. Not everybody is your customer. If your product is for everyone, it is actually for nobody. Why? Because if you cannot define the person, those people won't know your offering is for them. This is why you must define who they are, so that they know. You can't please everybody with your offering, and if you try to, it will most certainly result in business failure.

I have been in real estate since 2005. In that time, I have watched agents and brokers, who would have otherwise been successful, suffer, because they did not have a unique demographic. They tried to be all things to all people and ended up serving no one. Even in real estate, when you find what you are good at and you find a specific market, you go after that market. You do not try to be high-end homes, low-end homes, condominiums, new construction, resale; you do not try to do all of it. You try to find a specific market and target it. You should aim to become an expert in a certain field. The old sayings definitely hold true here, "Jack of all trades, master of none" and "When you appeal to everyone, you appeal to no one."

When it comes to niches, the last thing is to be aware of the 'evergreen niches'. These categories are timeless. That means there are always people looking for these types of products and services. There are the main three categories everyone falls into, in one way or another.

- Love and Romance

- Business and Money

- Health and Wellness

You do not have to fall into one of these categories exactly, but this is a head start. You can branch off into any number of niches or take one of these and narrow it down further - as Nerd Fitness did, even taking it a few levels deep.

These overarching categories are what most personal development, life and business programs fall under. You can branch off and create an entirely new niche as well. I have seen people sell $4,000 packages for intuition. It is completely up to you as long as you know your ideal market, and how to give them the transformation you are promising.

Multiple Niches

You might decide that your transformation could be applicable to several different niches, and that you could build a couple different customer avatars.

Whether it is okay to market to them all at once depends on what your program, service, course, book, live event, whatever your product really is. It depends on what your real solution and transformation is.

Is your ideal customer in two different niches? If they are, then target both those niches. However, you usually will find that you may actually have two different courses, two different programs, or two different products that you are trying to sell to two different types of people.

In that case, you can create variations of the same product. Whether it is a course, a book, a live event, or a mastermind, you can create variations of it. First, target one group, then target the other group with the other variation. Be sure to track what you do, and remember to do split testing to find out which one gets the best feedback.

The overall aim is to become the leader of your niche, to be the 'king of the hill'. You want to own that category. Do not compete; the reason we niche to a small group of people is to define our own category where there is no competition, and where we can lead. This is exactly what Nerd Fitness did – that category did not exist before they created it. The objective is to have your name or brand associated directly with what it is you are offering. When somebody says 'fast food', people think 'McDonalds'. When somebody thinks shipping, the answer is 'FedEx' and so on.

Customer Avatar

Once you have created your specific niche, the next step is to fully understand the individuals that make up that group. The way we get to know these individuals and their tastes is by creating a 'customer avatar'. A customer avatar is a specific person that represents your target market. For example, when starting out one of my membership sites, I created the name, age, gender, position, and normal, everyday life that this person would live. You really want to be specific with who this person actually is.

Once you have a customer avatar built, you will know their problems, their struggles, and exactly what would help them. You can then easily build a solution within your business to help them and know how to market directly to them. You can speak their language so that they understand that you have their specific solution. If you have a custom avatar built, you understand how they are thinking, feeling, where they are going, and all the things they do – day in and day out. You know specifically, how to target them and how to speak their language directly to them.

To create your customer avatar, first, you decide who your ideal customer is. What do they struggle with? What makes them happy? Where do they hang out online, and offline? Then, name them. Come up with actual names: Susan, Jessica, Zach, Dave etc. Decide their income level, their lifestyle; really create the person that you could help the most. Define what it is like in their life and what their problems are, what the solution would be to help them. Get to know him or her as if they were your friend, so you can find out the best way to serve them.

If you do not create a customer avatar, it would be like playing darts blindfolded and just throwing the darts everywhere. You are unlikely to hit the dartboard, and you are certainly not going to hit a bullseye. Your customer avatar is your bullseye – your ideal dream client. If you know who that is, you know where your bullseye lies and you can target it directly with your marketing, really hitting that bullseye over and over again. Otherwise, you are just throwing darts at a wall, all around the target, but never really hitting it at all.

It is impossible to build a program, service, course, or product for your customer if you do not truly understand who they are and what they struggle with. Without having your target audience well defined, you do not know where your dream clients are spending their time. On top of that, it would be difficult to market even the best products without knowing how to get in front of them.

Fishing Holes

Once you have identified who your ideal client is and have their avatar, the next step is to figure out where they spend their time. I refer to this as finding 'fishing holes'. A 'fishing hole' is where someone spends their time. The way to find out where their 'fishing hole' is begins with asking yourself some questions. If you were them, who would you follow online? Who are the gurus? Who are your favorite authors, the best-selling books you might read, the speakers you might follow, the public figures, and the authorities in your market? To whom would you look to for answers and advice?

When you start to figure out those things, you find out where they go to fish. Facebook or Google are great places to begin searching for those answers. You can find out what your customer avatar is looking at, what they are seeing, what people they are following. You will find out what pages they like, what Google searches they are looking for, what live events they attend, what books they read and so on.

Once you have your niche and your customer avatar built, then you can simply search for where these types of people would be. At this point you should know who their favorite authorities are, what Facebook pages they like, who they follow on Twitter, what Google searches they search for the most, because you understand them so well. Step two is to direct your marketing towards these areas. This is critically important because if you are in those places, to those people, you will look like you are everywhere. You will pop up in front of them as if you were the answer they had been searching for all along.

Narrowing Your Niche

Meditation:

- Who do you truly want to serve? Spend 10-20 minutes in quiet meditation reflecting on this.

- What do they do, how do they feel, how can you serve them to be greater?

Action Steps:

- Do above meditation.

- Narrow your niche by dividing up categories into subcategories.

- Define your customer avatar.

- Find your focus and ideal customer by defining where they work, what they do, how they feel, what they say, where they live, what Facebook pages they follow, what books they read, what videos they watch, who they follow, what they think and what they need the most help with.

CHAPTER 6

Craft Your Message & Offer

"The two words 'information' and 'communication' are often used interchangeably, but they signify quite different things. Information is giving out; communication is getting through."
— Sydney J. Harris

IDEALLY, AS AN ENLIGHTENED ENTREPRENEUR, your audience should be a previous version of you. Your message as well should be something you have learned, that has saved you from the pain you have struggled with, or the problem you had. Since they are a previous version of you, just look back on who you were before you solved the problem. Where were you mentally, emotionally, financially, spiritually? What were you searching for? How would a message have influenced you back then? What could someone have said that would have resonated with that older version of you?

Your clients want to know that you understand them. That you get what they are going through and that you have been through it too. They want to know that you can help them get through it, with compassion and understanding, because you have been through it already. Having a message that resonates will create the trust factor needed to make anyone your client. They know you get it and believe in you to solve the problem that they have.

Really, that is all that business is about: solving problems. It is about knowing more than the next person in your area of expertise knows. Without understanding the problems they face, you have no way of solving whatever they truly struggle with. You cannot create a business that way, unless you base it all off luck.

What Do You Do?

The other problem I see a lot of entrepreneurs have, is not being able to communicate what they do succinctly. Potential customers ask them what their product or service does and they stumble over their words as they try to explain it.

Here is a simple formula I use to help people be super clear about what transformation they help people with. "I help (specific type of person) to (outcome or transformation you help them achieve) by/through (coaching, online course, consulting etc.)."

So the formula becomes: I help X to Y by Z. For myself, I would say: I help heart-centered entrepreneurs to live out purpose driven lives by teaching them how to incorporate their passions into their business. I find this really helps tie together exactly what you are offering your niche.

I built Enlightenedentrepreneursacademy.com to address the frustration I saw in heart-centered entrepreneurs. They would buy every course, take every seminar and still struggle with how to launch, how to create an online course, how to be an author, how to be a coach or all the tech headaches that are required to actually make money doing what they love. I built this academy as a one-stop shop that makes sure they have somewhere to go, that has everything they need to start, build, grow and scale their businesses.

To find out your ideal audience's biggest struggles and problems to address, simply ask them. Reach out to people in your niche. Do not bombard them, but sincerely ask what they struggle with. As a solution, give your service or product out for free, at first, to a few people. Make sure you are truly solving the problem they are facing. This validates your idea and can give you great testimonials for when you are ready to launch.

You should know by now where to find your ideal client. You can find them on Facebook groups, on Google Hangouts, on Instagram, Twitter, and in different groups all over the Internet. Go ahead, join those groups, connect with people there, then begin to ask them what they are having problems with through being of service. Not necessarily just saying, "What do you struggle with?"

However, be vigilant to see what their problems are. Offer solutions and see if your solution is something that actually benefits them in the moment.

Freebies

Once you have discovered their real pain points, know the solution to their problem, and have created your product or service around it, then you can simply take one of the biggest pain points inside your solution and name your offer that.

Your offer or freebie that gets them involved, must be solution-based in its title and delivery. It solves one problem, leaving the solution to their bigger problem inside your product. Problem, solution. Problem, solution.

Your initial offer usually should come through some kind of freebie: a free webinar, a free e-book, a free three-part video series, a free course, a free e-mail sequence. You should title that freebie whatever your offer is. It should be the first problem that they have and the solution to it.

Your free course, or your free e-book, or your free download, or your free e-mail sequence, or video series, as Jeff Walker said, is your 'second best course'. Your first best course is what they pay for. Your second best is your free offer. Your freebie or offer should solve one little problem, leaving the bigger problem inside your course, program, live event, membership site, or mastermind, whatever it may be.

In your first offer or freebie, you have solved one of their problems for free. You have given them some valuable content. You have really helped them in a way that builds that trust, which builds your authority. They look to you for answers. They trust you and they believe in you. They know that if they pay for the upgrade, the actual product, or service, they are going to get even more value, because you gave away such good value in the free offer that you initially had.

SUMMARY 6

Craft Your Message & Offer

Meditation:

- Spend 10-20 minutes experiencing what your ideal customer experiences.

- Put yourself in their mind, heart, or position in life.

- To know them and their struggle is to know how to help them the most.

Action Steps:

- Do the above meditation.

- Write out all the feelings that your ideal client has.

- Write out all the words that come to mind for their transformation.

- Write out an advertisement with the above words that would appeal to your ideal client.

- What is the first problem you can solve for them, then the next?

- What is the free offer and what is the program?

CHAPTER 7

Creating Your System

"There is just no way of getting around it: You must allow yourself to be the Being that life is causing you to become if you are to feel joy. And unless you are feeling joy, you are not allowing yourself to be that which life has caused you to become."
-Abraham Hicks

TO REITERATE, ANY SYSTEM YOU CREATE as an Enlightened Entrepreneur should give a total transformation, no matter which way you deliver it. Whether it be via a book, course, program, coaching, or live event – the client should start from the version 1.0 of where they are, to the result or version 2.0 of where you are supposed to take them. Experience is truly all we ever have. Giving others an experience is the greatest thing you can pass on in business and in life. That is transformation; that is what you are selling – your gift.

You can sell a product, service, or package in any way you choose. But delivering a transformation is the highest form of them all. We do not know without a doubt why we are here, what the meaning of life is or what it truly means to be alive. All attempts at answering these hard questions are just beliefs and systems we have developed to help us cope with the profound idea that we do not know. However, what we do continually prove to ourselves, day in and day out, is that our experiences are real. The experience I am having writing this book or the experience you are having reading it.

Waking up, going to work, spending time with family, all these things are experiences. What better way to make a living than giving people experiences that provide transformation for them? In the end, it makes your life better knowing you gave them this gift, and it helps them transform to have a deeper experience themselves. When it comes to the business side of it, no one who experiences a true transformation through the service you provide will ever ask for a refund. Nothing but happy customers.

Working Backwards: Z to A

We want to develop a system for your offer, and we start with the end first.

- What is the end result?
- What is the transformation that they will have once finished?
- What will they think, feel, act, do, say, or experience, or have as a result of working with you - either one-on-one, in a group, or using your products or service?

Once you have answered these questions, you should work backwards to establish the milestones your client needs to reach in order to achieve the end result. What do they need to understand in order to get them to the next step in the process?

Breaking it down in this way and working backwards lays your system out in such a way that you give them what they need each step of the way, all the way to the finish line. Step by step. Module 1 gives them information, A. Then they should understand A. They get to Module 2, which is B; they know that they needed A to get to B, and they need B to get to C, all the way until their desired result. A to Z.

Results Based Systems

The key factor in what creates lasting success, or a perpetual stalemate, is your confidence in what you are providing. When you know your product or service delivers a transformation in a results-based system, you have every confidence to sell it for whatever price you determine. You have no issues in asking for what you know it is worth.

On the other hand, if you are hesitant to create, build, or launch your business, it is usually due to your lack of confidence or belief that you are of value.

Having a results-based system that gives a true transformation alleviates the pressure and allows for confidence.

If you do not have a clear system laid out with a big transformation as the result, you are cutting yourself off from the power of vision. Seeing the end goal and feeling it fully as if it is happening today is one of the greatest motivators. It will pull you to the finish line.

On top of that, if you do not know where you are taking your clients, you should not quite be in business yet. You should know what the goal is for them, what the goal is for yourself and the steps necessary for both parties to achieve the results you are aiming for.

You do not have to know your end goal in life, where you are going to be fifty years from now. However, you should have your transformational end goal - what you are providing to your clients - laid out in black and white, so you know how to take them there. Otherwise, you are not ready to be teaching, or coaching, or providing the service that you are promising.

On limitlessmasterminds.com, my membership site, the end result for every client is self-actualization. The initial thought when developing it was to upload all the content and take them through to self-actualization in three videos. Was that doing a service to my clients? Can someone truly self-actualize within hours? The honest answer, at least from my perspective, was "No."

No one can do that. It was going to be a disservice to them. I would in fact have given them the information to absorb, and subsequently forget, before they ever even had a chance to implement a single idea.

Instead, I implemented a results-based system. I broke it down into twelve modules: six main courses with multiple videos and exercises within each one. Then, six bonus modules to tackle specific areas of life: success and finance, relationships, productivity, and meditations. I added monthly group coaching calls as well, to make sure the freedom that I intended to give them followed the confusion they would experience as they break and rebuild lifelong-held beliefs.

Start with the end. Then work backwards to make sure they get the full experience that is promised.

Decide if it will take five steps, eight steps, twelve steps, three weeks, five months, or a year to get your client through their transformation. From 1.0 to 2.0. Then, decide how long each step will take them. Each step should build upon the last and give them what they need for the next step to make sense. It's important to deliver small wins along the way.

Small Wins

The concept of a 'small win' is that there are joyous moments amongst an activity or a period of time that is hard to get through or requires a lot of discipline and time. For example, when dieting, perhaps you are trying to get a six-pack, and you see one small line of definition on your abs. No, you do not have a full six-pack yet, but you experienced a small win and it gives you the motivation to continue along your journey.

Most people do not know what you know, and this can make it hard to impart your wisdom to them - the 'curse of knowledge'. The curse of knowledge is basically a cognitive bias that occurs when predicting others' forecasts or behaviors. We are unable to ignore the knowledge we have, incapable of disregarding information that we already possess, that others do not have. It makes it hard for you as the creator of the content to understand that those you teach do not have access to your life's experiences. You must make your content digestible, understandable, and easily consumable as your clients progress through each step.

Splitting your course up into a multi-part system with small wins for your client along the way gives them a constant lingering feeling of confidence. It allows them to believe fully that they can get the transformation they signed up for in the beginning.

Many people buy courses, training, coaching, or go to seminars and simply swallow the information –

but never take action of any kind. People spend and waste years and millions of dollars because they simply did not feel like they could actually achieve the transformation promised them themselves. Give them the wins and it will fuel them to continue, to actually take action and reach the finish line. If you are an Enlightened Entrepreneur, then you deeply care about your clients reaching the finish line.

If you were to sell your program or product without small wins for your client along the way, you could expect more refunds, confusion, and lack of trust from your clients, or an eventual end to the business itself. You would be better suited not to be in the field of being an Enlightened Entrepreneur, as it would mean shooting yourself in the foot and not really delivering the transformation that you need to.

Think about it: there are thousands of people that have bought tons of courses, who have never finished them. They have never gone all the way through each course because they never felt like they could really win. They never, ever felt like they could accomplish it. They did not have the confidence from those little wins to keep them motivated and engaged. They just felt like a kid with a fire hose in their face, getting information dumped on them at incomprehensible volumes. These people feel as if they were never actually able to digest and implement the content given to them, and take action.

In the end, what you want your clients to do is the same thing that I would want you to do: take action, move forward, and implement these things. Not just to read it, consume it, and understand it - but to take massive action, day in and day out. Get up, try, do, act and make it happen.

Creating Your System

Meditation:

- Spend 10-20 minutes in meditation experiencing the transformation you will be delivering to your ideal client. How will they think, act, feel and be when they are done?
- Spend 10-20 minutes meditating on being paid what you're worth.

Action Steps:

- Do the above meditations.
- Define your transformation.
- Is it 5, 8, 12 modules, weeks, months, years?
- Is it an online course, coaching program, book, mastermind or live event?
- What is the win they experience at week 1, 2, 3...?
- What will be the cost of not working with you for them?

- Define your price point, initial offer and upsell. Allow more into your life financially.

CHAPTER 8

Value Proposition

"That's the heart of this entire concept. Clients do not buy 'things'. They buy the experiences that those 'things' are able to deliver. And, when so doing, they measure the benefits against the costs. Which leads us directly to consider: what is a value proposition?"

— Cindy Barnes

YOUR UNIQUE VALUE PROPOSITION is about what unique value you can deliver to your client. It is why they should go on their transformation with you, rather than another person. What makes you different? The crux of the matter is - you are the one who will be selling your product or service. What do you offer that nobody else does? Building your product or service based on an incredible value will give you the ability to sell with much more confidence and ease.

After you make any sale, while you are delivering your product or service, you can be confident that your client will be satisfied. Having your niche narrowed down, knowing your customer avatar, developing your results-based system, giving your client the true transformation – all these add up to having a value that is uniquely yours. Your market will notice this value, and your customers will appreciate any authenticity you add.

Being unique separates you from the masses. There are millions of coaches, courses, programs, services, which millions of different people provide. You do not need to completely reinvent the wheel, but having your own special touch on your service will make it that much more valuable to the clients you are helping.

Being unique will also assist in attracting your ideal customers, who will only want to work with someone as unique as you are. You are your own best customer. They will be attracted to you because of your authenticity and the unique value that you deliver.

Focus on what it is you give that others do not. When it comes to the technology or the structure, it can be hard to differentiate. However, when it comes to their transformation, only you can provide what is unique to you and your client.

You have a gift; you have a calling – something that is special to you. There is a way of looking at the world that only you see – a way of processing your experience that only you have. You have this within you, and the world is waiting for it to come out. Do not hold back from giving your gift to the thousands of people that are waiting to benefit from your message. You are who you have been waiting for.

Summary 8
Your Value Proposition

Meditation:

- Spend 10-20 minutes experiencing the value you provide.

- Free yourself of programing and allow what it is you truly add to the world to come forth.

Action Steps:

- Define the value you provide to others.

- Reiterate to yourself what the cost of them not working with you is.

- What are the benefits to their life now and in the long term if they do work with you?

- How would the world look if you could truly transform everyone in this way?

- What is the cost to the world of you not delivering this value to them?

PART 3

Action

Ac·tion

/ˈakSH(ə)n/

noun

The fact or process of doing something, typically to achieve an aim.

CHAPTER 9

Motivation

"Do you want to know who you are? Don't ask. Act!
Action will delineate and define you."
— Thomas Jefferson

"Of course motivation is not permanent. But then,
neither is bathing; but it is something you should do on
a regular basis."
— Zig Ziglar

Now it's all good and well to know what it is you are selling, to know what transformation it is you want to give and to whom. Yet, knowing these things is not enough. As has been repeated many times, action is the key to success. What is it that pushes you past that learning threshold into actually doing? Motivation.

To be motivated is to have a reason or desire to act or do something. It is your driver; what pushes and pulls you forward. Motivation is the gas in the engine that will make your car run.

You could have turned yourself from a beat-up old car to a red Ferrari through extensive self-improvement. Maybe you are parked on the racetrack and you know where you have to go in business and in life because you have thoughtfully mapped it out in advance. It is great to be in this circumstance; but the reality is you need the gas, the drive, the motivation to continue driving every day to get to your destination. It's the missing link.

Motivation is not just something you wake up with. Most people are not blessed with infinite amounts of drive. You can control your own levels of motivation by digging deep, finding your why, and by focusing your time properly. You have total and complete control over everything you say, act and do – including your determination and drive.

It may be hard to accept this as fact, that you have full control over your own motivation. People do not want to acknowledge this as a fact because it requires them to take on full responsibility for all their actions, including their motivation levels. However, it is only through this acceptance that you gain true power.

It can be hard, for sure. Always staying motivated is a skill, a conscious act and it can be draining. Life is not always going to be rosy. Things come up, setbacks happen. It is because of the reality of these setbacks that we need to learn to foster our own motivation, and not to rely upon others to pep us up every time. If you do not have an inner drive, then each setback has the ability to stop you in your tracks completely. You must dig deep to find what motivates you even in the face of adversity.

Keeping yourself going no matter what happens will be the determinant between what goals you make your reality, and what continues to stay but a dream. As Napoleon Hill said, "Action is the true measure of intelligence."

If you cannot create a structure that supports your motivation, you will always be easily distracted from your main objectives. Life can effortlessly become one big distraction if you let it. You must schedule your time. Set aside minutes, hours and days for you to do what it is you know you need to do. Having a structure and system in place to continue on your set tasks will keep you from derailing off track when things get busy.

Find Your Why

An important aspect of maintaining your own levels of motivation is to find your unique 'Why'. Your Why must be bigger than you. It must stretch beyond any single person or situation. Think of what you would do if everyone approved of you. What if no one else could influence you or deter you off the path you want to live. What would you chase that is bigger than your own life?

Many people use others as their Why. Although this can work temporarily, I believe it burns out eventually. Taking actions just to please others is a slippery slope to repression and guilt. This is why your meaning must come from your authentic self. Ask: "What is the legacy I want to leave in this world?"

If you could attend your own memorial at the end of your life, what would you want your friends, family and acquaintances to say about you? What is left behind, what has changed, because of your impact on the world? What is the difference you want to make? What is the experience you wish to leave here?

It is essential you know your Why, in order to define your end goal in business and in life. Always start with the end in mind. The end holds the vision for you. It is the overall big picture, the results, the experience you will create for yourself and others. This may change over time; it may become larger or smaller. Start right now with the biggest vision you can imagine and then work backwards.

As an example, I always buy yearly calendars. I start by marking off my vacation times first; my planning times second, then work in each goal by months, then weeks, then days. Starting with the end goal in mind allows me to break it down into smaller, actionable steps that can build to create the result I want.

Ironically, I even plan the experiences that I want to have happen spontaneously. I set aside time with family, with friends, or for when I want to create content, to just free-flow in the moment. These times are free but planned. When I do not plan my free-flow time, I usually find that I am distracted during those periods. I might want to spend quality time with my family, but if I do not set aside a specific time for that, I end up being distracted thinking about work when the chance does arise.

You should plan you free-flow time, your family time, your creative time, and your marketing time. When you see on your calendar that it is now time to do a certain activity, you should aim to be present, fully. Undistracted.

New Achievements

So, after you have set your end goals and have planned all your steps out on the calendar, what happens when you achieve your goal? The glory of goal-setting is that life does not end when you eventually complete your set task. Each accomplishment unlocks a new achievement. You can set improved goals. Often, the higher you reach, the different your goals become. Once you reach a goal you set 6 months ago, you might be a completely different person with a completely new set of standards and goals.

Most entrepreneurs start out wanting to make money. Now, this is not inherently a bad goal! Money is simply energy; it is a tool to use to make life what you wish it to be. However, after you make money, you might shift your sights to making a certain impact instead of a certain income. Eventually, you will want to be remembered, and then it becomes about impact and leaving a legacy for the world at large.

Just as we follow Marlow's hierarchy of needs, we start with our own wants, then gradually, as we fulfill each one, we shift to yearning to make more of a difference in the world. As an enlightened entrepreneur, you want to start with both yourself and the world – to make income through your impact.

Summary 9

Motivation

Meditation:

- What is your Why?
- What do you really want? What would you do if everyone said yes?

Action Steps:

- Do the above meditation for 20 – 30 minutes.
- Write out your answers to the questions below:
- What is the legacy you wish to leave in this world?
- If there was a memorial for you at the end of your life, what would you want your friends, family and acquaintances to say about you?
- What is left behind, what has changed, as a result of your impact on the world?
- What is the difference you want to make?

- What is the experience you wish to leave here?

CHAPTER 10

Success Rituals

"Your beliefs become your thoughts,
Your thoughts become your words,
Your words become your actions,
Your actions become your habits,
Your habits become your values,
Your values become your destiny."
— Mahatma Gandhi

So, what is the secret to unending motivation, to achieving goals and overall success? Good habits. A habit is simply a repeated behavior that has gone unchecked for a period, which eventually becomes second nature to you.

When you are first learning to drive a car you have to think about each motion - the mirrors, gas, brake, possibly the gear stick. Now, I can bet that most of you reading this, given that you are older than 18, drive as a habit. You do all the motions it takes to start, drive and park your car as second nature. This is you on autopilot. Many people are on autopilot with most habits in their lives. They continuously do repeated behaviors without consciously thinking about any of the actions.

Who we are, is really just a series of habit loops on repeat. These habits happen to make up who we are, how we spend our time and what we achieve on this earth.

The habits you are currently displaying could have been learned behaviors from family, friends, school or society, often acquired unconsciously. However, we cannot blame our past for our current actions. You are in control of every action in your own life, and it is now your own responsibility to edit the habits that do not help you move forward.

Bad habits are those repeated, autopilot behaviors that cause harm to your life, your body, your money, your time, your family or business. If your favorite television show, food or bit of escapism is taking time, money or energy away from what is truly important in your life, then you know it has become a bad habit. Your kids could probably use your attention over that ball game; your business could probably use your money more than that nice pair of shoes. Writing your next best-selling book or launching your new course is definitely a better way to spend the time than you did watching the latest television show over the last 6 months.

If you have identified some (or numerous) bad habits in your life, then you need to think hard about what you could replace them with instead. First, you must know your Why, as earlier discussed. Know your reason for doing anything in your life. Have your goals written down, preferably into your yearly calendar. If you have worked backwards to get to actionable steps, then you will know how much time should be spent on each of your goals. Decide to replace your autopilot habits with new habits that will accomplish the dreams you have set out to undertake.

Think of a time when a habit you did not realize was bad, was actually hurting you in some way. At any level of awareness, there are things you fail to realize. It took me a few years to realize how my body reacts to an unhealthy diet. I have always had a sweet tooth. Even though I knew sugar was not good for me, it took years for me to consciously realize the negative impact it had on my moods, energy level, productivity, and sleep – to name a few. Take a mental inventory of all your habits every few months, and decide whether they are pushing you forward or – more likely – holding you back from being your best self.

Popular belief among experts is that it takes 21 days to form a new habit. For smaller habits, this might hold true. To mold larger habits, however, it can take you 60 days or more.

First, you must identify the habits you wish to remove. Write down the thoughts associated with this old habit, the feelings you experienced and the actions you took. This will help you identify when you are slipping back into your old habit, and will bring it into your conscious awareness, out of autopilot mode.

Now, replace the old habits you identified with new ones. Habits that are more desirable for the life you choose to have. Each day, when you would normally be in that old habit, make a conscious choice to adopt a new, more helpful habit instead. Start small, and start with one habit. Trying to take on and change everything you have ever been addicted to will be a sure-fire recipe for disaster.

Morning Rituals

A common attribute many hugely successful executives possess is their daily success rituals. A daily success ritual starts with your morning routine. Most people wake up and the first thing they do is roll over and check their phone – before they have even wiped the sleep out of their eyes. They dive right into email or Facebook before filling their mind with nutrients. Your daily success ritual should be the first few hours of your day. This will set the foundation for a great, fulfilling, successful day.

Personally, I wake up, make a quick juice, do a small amount of exercise and then read something powerful. I fill my mind and body with what I want to become, first. You can watch a positive video, read or take any action that fills you up first. I eat breakfast, review my day and plan my top priorities. All of this happens before I check my email, respond to messages or engage with any work.

Laying a solid foundation for a great day encourages you to start the day on a positive note, and then continue in this constructive fashion. You will be less tempted to let that one event turn your entire day into a 'terrible day', if anything occurs that might throw you off. I focus my first few hours on accomplishing the most important tasks, and then handle the items remaining.

Habit Factor

Morning rituals work well only when they become habits. If you focus those first few hours in the morning on getting your mind, body and heart right, then accomplishing the things you deem as top priority will be easy – because this action becomes habitual.

What's more? You will continue to have further success faster, as a few hours a day of high-impact work coming from a clear head space can add up to the equivalent of more than 21 additional days per year. In these high-impact hours, you can accomplish 4-5x more than you would be able to in the same amount of time, if you were distracted.

Tony Robbins has a morning routine he has coined his 'Hour of Power'. He suggests everyone set up their own Hour of Power, which involves light exercise, motivational incantations and at least 10 minutes of thinking of everything you are grateful for. Robbins then says to visualize everything you want in your life, as if you had it today. With this powerful start to every morning, you will be focused, open-hearted and positive from the get-go. Look at any successful athlete or businessperson; they invest their mornings into building a strong set of expectations for their day.

Letting your mornings go unchecked can lead to a domino effect. Imagine you wake up and go straight into your email. There, you find someone else's emergency – which immediately pulls you into reactive mode. You are now basing your priorities on other people's schedules. This responsive behavior will place you in fear mode, dragging you through the day being reactive rather than being proactive. This downward spiral continues to keep you stuck.

If your day starts this way, then when you come up against something difficult - a hurdle in your day - you will be more likely to give up and fail to meet your goals.

The number one fear contributing to people's resistance to setting up their own morning rituals is the feeling of being bogged down by discipline. It feels too controlled and rigid. The truth is - it is in discipline and consistency that you will find freedom. Setting yourself up with a proper routine of successful rituals pays dividends through the freedom of more time off and the ability to have a clear mind. Being consciously unaware of your autopilot habits is the real lack of control and destroys your freedoms.

Time Blocking

So how do you set up a morning a ritual for yourself? Time blocking. Time blocking is exactly what it sounds like. You block out a period to focus strictly on one particular task. Set your schedule to either hours, days or weeks and block out the time needed for a single task. Do not let anything else get in the way - especially other people's priorities. Do not let them take away from your task or let anything become a part of your day that has not already been planned to be there. If you do not make your own plan, you will become a part of somebody else's.

During your morning ritual, block out the first two hours of your day for the highest priority items. Decide what to spend one hour on and focus solely on that one task. You can watch, as your mind will want to wander or think of other things, distracting you. You will see how other people's priorities try to take your attention away. Bring your attention back to your current assignment, and practice focus.

Being present in the moment is difficult for many people; time blocking helps you learn discipline in this. When you have completed your hour, or your set task, release that task from your mind. Focus now on your family or other activities. Be present with them as well. As time goes on it, will become second nature to pour 100% of your attention into whatever you are doing in that moment.

Time blocking and staying present is extremely important in today's attention-deficit-driven society. It is easy for every new shiny object you perceive to distract you. This gives the power to the environment around you. Time blocking allows you to take the power back, free yourself from the addiction to your surroundings, and helps you ignore the shiny lights of new notifications.

Time blocking is key to being productive and a huge factor for our success. It is a mental and emotional cleanse from modern society's constant pull for our attention.

Prioritization

When you are time blocking, you need to pick the most important tasks to do in your morning ritual. When choosing which tasks you place at a higher priority, think about the 80/20 rule. The essence of this rule is that you generally get 80% of your desired outcomes from 20% of your time and effort. Prioritizing will help you focus on that 20% that is giving you the most.

Write out everything you have to do and make a note of the results you wish to accomplish. Then figure out which of those items is a 'need-to-do'. A lot of the 'busy' work we fill our time up with is not actually necessary to realize our end goal. All the fluff simply makes us feel like we are getting things done, when in reality, we are wasting 80% of our time, reaping only 20% of the benefits.

If you want to figure out which task is most important, a useful question I ask myself is 'Which of these tasks, when complete, will render the others on my list as unnecessary or easier?' This is called a focusing question. This, along with the hardest, most difficult or scary task is the best place to begin your day.

Success Ritual

Meditation:

- "What is the one thing that you could do that by so doing would eliminate everything else?"
  – Gary Keller

Action Steps:

- Build your morning ritual.
- What are the first things you will do in the morning? What will you eat, watch, read, and do to prepare yourself for a success day?
- Set up your time blocking schedule. What will the first hour of your day contain? What will be in your next high impact hour?
- Buy your yearly calendar and schedule in everything you want to manifest.
- Write out what the 20% is in your life and work that gives you 80% of your results.

Conclusion

"It is the depth of your consciousness that will determine your capacity for experience."
- Corey Gladwell

WHAT WOULD IT BE LIKE TO HAVE all aspects of your life completely aligned? To feel completely yourself all the time? For your work, leisure and family time to be one? To experience the freedom you always dreamed of? To have no more separation between what you do for a living and who you are as a person? That is what life is like for an Enlightened Entrepreneur.

By now, you should understand your purpose, the experiences you want to give and receive in life and so, in business. You have learnt the skills to be able to identify, break your old limiting beliefs and to override them with new ones.

You have narrowed down your niche, and have built up your customer avatar as if you knew him or her as a friend, inside and out. You know how to find the market your ideal clients are in. You know where exactly to find them so that you can appear in front of the right people, at the right time, through the right medium, and with the right message.

You should have a system outlined that you know will produce great results for your clients because the system is based on real experience and past problems, which you have solved.

Lastly, and arguably most importantly, you should be prepared to begin your morning ritual, which focuses you and adds many productive hours into each of your days.

Applying only a fraction of what you have learned throughout this book has the potential to take you on the ultimate fulfilling life journey.

The information included in this book is worth thousands. It literally cost me thousands to learn and to garner all of this knowledge, just like it costs most entrepreneurs to learn all these different elements. All of this can take you far - as long as you implement what you have learnt.

You now have all the information you need to get started pursuing your passion business and earning income through impact. If you are like me, however, you want fast results, you want to excel quicker and move to the next level without having to go through trial and error on your own. Simply put, you want a proven model and a system to follow.

That is why I have developed my exclusive program, enlightenedentrepreneursacademy.com.

This program is for the enlightened, heart-centered entrepreneur who truly wants to make a difference in the lives of their clients while making a wealth of income for themselves.

Included inside it is everything you need from start to finish. We dive deeper into the practical details of each aspect taught in this book. We delve into the details of it all: how to create online courses, how to become a published author, how to run a results-based coaching business – to name a few. The most difficult part to perfect for most people is the technology side needed to bring in clients on demand, whenever you want them. This course will take care of this aspect for you.

If you are - or would like to be - an author, coach, course creator or enlightened entrepreneur, then this is the only course you will require. It is the first and the last place you will ever need to go to, in order to make your success a reality.

Whoever you are, wherever you are at on this journey, understand that I have been there. I have lived at one extreme, owning a million-dollar business, and I have been at the other, nearly homeless. I have seen and experienced everything in-between.

Life is a journey. It is about this experience you are having. Regardless if you and I get the opportunity to work together or not, I want nothing but the best for you, and I truly do love you as I do my own family.

I want success and fulfillment for each person in this world. To have the experience of being independent, full, whole, complete, satisfied and truly free.

That is why I have written this book – to give individuals the tools necessary to create a business living in alignment with the soul of who they are. I want you to have an experience here on earth that is one to remember. After all, it is the depth of your consciousness that will determine your capacity for experience.

Learn, live, love and experience.

Bonus Chapters

How to Meditate

IT IS POSSIBLE TO MEDITATE AT any point in the day, but most people choose to do so either first thing in morning or at night before they go to bed. The benefit of the morning is that you can add it to your morning success ritual and set a good foundation for the day ahead. The benefit of the evening before bed is that it is a good way to unwind before getting a good night's rest. You could even decide to meditate both in the morning and in the evening; but remember that consistency is key – do not overwhelm yourself at first or you are more likely to give up.

The length of your meditation can be anywhere from 10 minutes, up to 2 hours. Many people start at smaller increments of time, and as they see the benefits of the meditation taking hold on their life, they naturally increase the time they spend in meditation.

To begin, find a quiet area - a room without distraction of light or noise. You can either sit erect or lay down flat on the bed or ground. Some people fall asleep if they lie down, so you may want to try sitting up erect.

After you have positioned yourself and you are ready to begin, simply close your eyes and relax your body. Take a few deep breaths, inhaling fully into your body. Feel yourself: your arms, your legs, your heart. Breathe into your body and become aware of the space around it. Allow your mind to run free with every thought that surfaces, yet simply realize that you are not your thoughts. You are, instead, the observer watching the thoughts pass by in your mind. Just watch as your mind conjures up anything and everything. Become aware - become present. Watch, observe and allow it to be.

If you find yourself caught up in your thoughts, simply acknowledge that your ego mind is showing you what you are resisting. Say thank you for it showing you what you are resisting, then step back into the observer again and watch.

How to Break Limiting Beliefs

Limiting beliefs can be extremely obvious at times, but more often than not, they stay well hidden. They stay disguised as a moral compass, or as the notion that you are being the good boy or girl your parents raised you as. They hide as a form of standing up for what you "believe" in. Many times our limiting beliefs keep us from even seeing them.

Your level of happiness, income, love, joy and fulfillment is entirely set by what you currently believe is possible for you to attain.

An example is of my own income levels. When I was young, I grew up poor and my life was hard. It was not hard simply because we were poor, but because of the lifestyle we were surrounded with. The moment we moved to a better neighborhood and our family was no longer surrounded by negativity, we began to move up toward a normal, average American life. In my Child Mind, I associated being poor to having a bad life.

So my pursuit of money began. I chased it as if it was the answer, the solution to having a good life. I never addressed the effects of the negative lifestyle we grew up in since I simply equated it to a lack of money. Eventually, as you read in my introduction, I gained the money I thought would solve all my problems – yet it all came crashing down.

At this point, my income diminished to zero. When I had my enlightenment, I experienced more love, joy, fulfillment and complete peace than I had ever previously experienced - with or without money. Something in my mind clicked.

The money, whether having it or not, did not equate to my level of fulfillment, happiness, love or freedom. What truly created my experience of life was my internal state. This was the first step to uncovering what limiting beliefs I had held all those years about money – but it did not end there.

I began to conduct an experiment with myself around my belief systems that I share with my clients and will share with you now as well.

Breaking Beliefs Experiment:

I wrote out everything I believed. Every belief that I had about money, time, love, family, friendship, business, freedom, life and all that it included.

- Money equals freedom
- Love means sacrificing yourself for another
- You have to trade your time for money
- Once I have the life I want, I'll be free
- Business is cut-throat

- Family means you must take care of them before yourself
- Something else is in charge of my life

Then I took all those beliefs and wrote down the complete opposite of them; another belief but its opposing view.

- Freedom equals money (When I'm free the money will follow)
- Love means taking care of yourself first
- You don't have to trade time for money
- Once I'm free I'll have the life I want
- Business is peaceful, kind and caring
- Family means you must take care of yourself in order to be an example of what self-love is for them
- I am in charge of my life

I read the list of beliefs, the ones I had and the counter arguments to them as well. I fully realized that both lists were just beliefs, and that neither one is necessarily right or wrong. Both are simply beliefs.

I reread them slowly and noticed which ones made me feel fuller. Which ones made me come alive, feel lighter and happier, more excited and passionate. I understood that I did not need to believe either one, but could choose to believe anything I wanted to.

My beliefs are not me. My religion is not me. My thoughts are not me. My version of reality, my perspective is not me. I am much larger than all of these things, yet I am still human with a set of beliefs.

So the question became, which set of beliefs serves me greater? Which set of beliefs makes me come alive? Which belief makes me fall more in love with the human experience? I choose to go with that belief.

The results are the incredible life I have today, both inside and out. The beauty of this exercise is that it is not the last time I, or more clients, have used it. Every time my clients come up against something in their lives and they do not know which way to go, what to believe or what decision to make, I simply ask them to do this exercise. Which belief will serve them greater?

Breaking your perception, unlocking the grip from your beliefs is a freedom most people do not get to experience. Having the full knowledge deep within yourself that you have the complete freedom to change everything you think, feel, do or say at any time is a power most will not even let themselves experience. Many people intentionally keep this power hidden from themselves because it is such an unknown concept, and the resulting belief about it creates fear.

The present reality we live in is full of a freedom that many do not see. The world blinds them with what it wants them to believe, by what is forced onto us as children and indoctrinated in us as adults. The truth is, the reality we live in is based on beliefs, and the only question is whose beliefs are we going to base it off?

If you think there is any difference between you and the life you want, between you and the person you wish to become, between you and all the dreams you've ever had - then this exercise is for you.

If you have always had everything you want in love, money, business, relationships and personal fulfillment, then you are already experiencing the freedom that comes from adopting your true belief system.

In the end, you are free to choose any beliefs you want about your life, yourself and the story you have created about them both.

So, I'll leave you with the question to ask yourself next time you don't know what to do:

Who would I be without that thought?

About the Author

Best-Selling Author Corey Gladwell is a speaker and coach who has built his knowledge of entrepreneurship and the path to enlightenment on a lifetime's experience. After struggling on section 8 and welfare when he was young. Corey grew an intense desire to succeed. By age 23 Corey owned a nightclub, his own vodka brand and a restaurant, all of which were highly prosperous, only to self-sabotage his own success. After experiencing a spiritual awakening where he was able to connect with the oneness of all life, he now runs a wildly successful business leading others to the freedom they desire through personal and financial transformations. Corey shares with us how to actualize the self through all mediums, specifically focusing on how to make an income in a way that follows your purpose. He gives the heart-centered entrepreneur practical, realistic actions to prevent themselves from feeling emptiness so that they can have lasting success. Corey has also written the bestseller The Human Experience: A Guide to Personal Fulfillment, Meaningful Worth and Ultimate Awareness. To find out more about Corey, visit www.coreygladwell.com

www.ingramcontent.com/pod-product-compliance
Lightning Source LLC
Chambersburg PA
CBHW032033050726